Sorrow's
Kitchen

Also by James Sallis

Novels

The Long-Legged Fly
Moth
Black Hornet
Eye of the Cricket
Bluebottle
Death Will Have Your Eyes
Renderings

Short Story Collections

A Few Last Words
Limits of the Sensible World
Time's Hammers: Collected Stories

Nonfiction

Chester Himes: A Life
Difficult Lives
Gently into the Land of the Meateaters
Ash of Stars: On the Writing of Samuel R. Delany *(editor)*
Saint Glinglin by Raymond Queneau *(translator)*
The Guitar Players
Jazz Guitars *(editor)*
The Guitar in Jazz *(editor)*

Forthcoming

Ghost of a Flea *(novel)*
Black Night's Gonna Catch Me Here: Selected Poems 1968–1998

Sorrow's Kitchen

poems by **James Sallis**

Michigan State University Press
East Lansing

∞The paper used in this publication meets the minimum requirements of
ANSI/NISO Z39.48–1992 (R 1997) (Permanence of Paper).

Michigan State University Press
East Lansing, Michigan 48823-5202

Printed and bound in the United States of America.

07 06 05 04 03 02 01 00   1 2 3 4 5 6 7 8 9 10

LIBRARY OF CONGRESS CATALOGING-IN-PUBLICATION DATA

Sallis, James, 1944–
    Sorrow's kitchen : poems / by James Sallis.
       p.   cm.
    ISBN 0–87013–562–7 (alk. paper)
    I. Title.
    PS3569.A462 S67 2000
    811'.54–dc21

                                                          00–008803

Individual poems have appeared in *Poetry East, Transatlantic Review, Negative
Capability, The Widener Review, High Plains Literary Review, Slipstream, North
Dakota Quarterly, South Dakota Review, Black Warrior Review, Karamu, Ascent,
Oasis, New Mexico Humanities Review, The Poetry Review, The Literary Review,
Extensions, Open Places, The Chariton Review, Manhattan Poetry Review, The
Dickinson Review, Eratica, The Portland Review,* and *New Orleans Review.*

Cover artwork is "Still Life with Earthquake" and is used by permission of
the artist, Elisabeth Garrett Spragg.

Cover and text design by Michael J. Brooks

_____

Visit Michigan State University Press on the World Wide Web at:
                www.msu.edu/unit/msupress

To Dave Lunde

Contents

Memory's Empire

Such abandon! you said when I offered
my back, a thing of little worth,
to bring us closer. On the shelf
by forgotten books where we slept,
you curled about your dreams
of corners and curves.

Snow threw itself into huddles,
like a troubled child, outside our window:
an economy of endings.

Now I have left your bed, taking along
all my names and quiet departures.
You push at the borders of silence,
that shabby suburb. Blood surrounds
air whistling within you: tonight,
because of rain, you cannot breathe.

2.

Slowly night let us know her.
To your body
I came wide-eyed and without words,
as into foreign lands.

In alleys there, red pianos carried on
pursuing their prey,
gobbling down with Mozart and Brahms
the helpless, homeless.

In cramped market stalls not far
from our apartment
we bought two paintings, half a pound
of music, a bag of brightly wrapped stories.

Light here is different, you said. Children
trailed behind us down twisting streets,
their small heads sinking again
and again into blue, yellow, sky.

3.

Had you noticed? you say:
there's more sky. As rain
gathers like a word that finally may explain
what happens down here.

My dear, I have been unfaithful,
the Baron tells his wife. In the pale
yellow gaslight of my laboratory,
out of the loins of my need, from knowledge
and love of knowledge,
I have made a son that is not yours.

4.

Our radios announce again
the old disasters, ancient failures
of language and will.

If only sky might accept us,
would deliver us
from this dull earth rolling like a pig
who will eat them
on the axis of its young.

5.

I was speeding to Conclusions
(just outside Taos) when I came upon you there
on spongy asphalt staring down the sun.

I had packed away all ambition.
Your life was as plain and self-contained
as the cactus it stepped from.

We rolled towards hills like loaves of bread
beneath the sun, a smell
of fresh earth rising from your body.

Heat and light beat about us there
like heavy wings
bearing up, about to become
visible, about to come into being.

3

6.

The mornings of your life
gather like crows:
you cannot keep them away.

Shuddering with anticipation
in its harbor, the ship keeps count
of bodies walking into it.

Because I can no longer raise
the questions,
because I cannot support
truth or its widower's eyes,

now I will be flame,
the young man says.

7.

Ardent reason, please forgive me.
You must know by now
that I will not be coming back.
Still I care deeply, each night
carry photos of you to bed
where sleep waits
with its luminous scrapbook.

Your face rose over the dark horizon
of a coffee cup. Wet
with a decent happiness, you said,
yes, but mind: what you carry
away from here, you will carry
in bottomless boxes,
ever the lighter for it.

8.

Borne up by my silence
you cross the borders into light.
Sky has become water for you, rain,

and memory's flame at play between us
burns green, bright green,
with the copper of earth and setting suns.

At night by the fire, in your green eyes
I read again this story of ruin:
how hope has moved away
and desire lives alone,

here in this country where
only the past shows in mirrors.

Nine Below Zero

Today a man died on the street. They say
the bullets spread their soft hands
    across his skin like words
and urged it open. Collapsing off the stone
    side of the building
where the loud gun had thrown him,
a corridor appeared in him all at once,
    the size
of a finger. He gave birth to a vacuum,
that sucked his bowels out onto the street
    near Macy's.
The wall behind him slammed by a red fist;
    pebbles, plaster
falling into him. The manager calls the police,
    an ambulance,
and then the workmen. They can come tomorrow.

Today a man died on the street. They say
it was terrible. It makes evening headlines;
    TV coverage
shows him lying inside himself on the sidewalk,
    dead, people
in crowded rings watching. And him, the other
    (they say
he was like that for an hour) standing still
    with the gun
limp in his hand, and smiling.

Today a man died on the street. At Broadway
        and 34th,
3 P.M. on a warm day, the 3rd of December —
but what of it? Why all this bother?

Just that one man is empty
and done with listening to others; and another
finally found a way to speak, to say
all the things he wanted, dumb for years.

Here

Here
the people
echo defeat.

They have fallen
to disease,
a disease,
some thing that makes

the marrow fluid, so it pours
out of their
bones as though they were
drinking straws.

Wind
catches in the empty bones.
A different sound
for each bone.

The bones
empty,
bending,

even
the best cannot
stand
upright now.

Prayer

Father,
they are peeling his
eyeball, revolving

his eye between
thumb and forefinger,
slowly. The white

drops thin and clinging
from the potato
slicer, the merest film
of mucous on formica.

Father, they
are planting his
naked eye. It disappears

like a wink
in the soil of the windowbox
under cupped
and shaping hands.

Father,
forked dry twigs
like the veins of eyes

are reaching
out of the mound. Father,
the trees
are filled with eyes.

How to Save Them

Come in half-dressed
holding a grand piano in one hand.

You cannot tell them
what you had in mind, but you can allow
questions and if they come close,
pass out small prizes.

When it is your turn, ask them
how much they will charge you
to become angels. Explain to them
how important this is to you.

Ask them to tell you in their own words
what the following statement means:

The text must prove to me
that it desires me.

What You Must Take with You

Hair of the dog   because your memory will not be good
                         there

A rose   because you will have to eat

Family photos   so you will not have to travel alone

Snow   you will need it to carry your things in

Candles   to pay your way

Desire   you will have use of it
                         there

Erotics of Early Morning

1.

In your absence I watch young lovers
next door quarrel, moving
in fits, in starts, across stained asphalt.

They lean again and again
into their leaving, reeled back by words.

The world has become a negative of their desire,
an impression, an emptiness.

2.

The world, say, is a woman
who knows you desire her.
At night past the chill pane of your window
she displays herself: breast flattened
beneath one hand, bump of a hip
against someone, something, not there.

3.

From my hands you
empty out into the world's mouth.
I scoop you up again.
You pour away and are gone.

A Marriage

You always preferred, I remember,
even then, the ridge of the eyes.
Washington was your favorite — the high
forehead, nose like a flat fish —

and for me it was Lincoln:
cheekbone arc de triomphe, jaw
shaped like a couch
and cheeks sunk just enough

to push back into and sit there.

Our shoes bit into the upper lip
and we tiptoed to reach up into
the nostrils, where a hard liver-colored

fungus grew; finally broke off
one small piece. You carried it

from my palm to your lips. They closed
around it. It was good;
savory, nourishing.

And now we sleep in ears, eyes,
where teeth should be — curled up
under the curve of lips, each asleep
in the hammock of an eyelid.

The mushrooms are yellow,
and your hair turns color before
the seasons, pulling them along.

Our trips down
across the front of the face
grow rarer each week now.

We hate descent of any sort
and have filled our shoes
with belonging. We grow thin,
like birds who used to come here.

Features blur with time.
We look down at the gravel of
eyes, cheeks, noses, eyes,
where teeth should be. We are content.

My Job

When I got there, there weren't many left
There was a hole in the wall
They showed it to me and said, That's
Where they went through

It wasn't much larger than a fist
You have to think about all of them
Going in there
No idea what's at the end
Not even sure there is one

That's where they went through

You have to think about that
If it was courage, faith, habit

Going in there with no idea
What's at the end
Branches, tunnels, hollows
And the rest holding back now
Looking in, feet on the edge

Don't do it, I tell them
They pay me for that

Home Movies

The window looks on
to watch our
turnings
here in this bed,
five by four,
hole in the sky.

Night comes
and the window's a mirror
crossed by two wood stakes.

We eat garlic, listen
to scrapings on the roof.

Other Conclusions

It was always endings he loved,
nudging blindly towards them, as
into a pillow, the way they'd
come spilling up over the prow,
as surprised as he was.

Last lines of old books, bittersweet ends
of brief affairs, memory lingering
as twilight blushed into evening.
Learning to close doors on rooms of his life
he'd not be coming back to.

Only endings allowed things to stay
as they were, as they had been:
otherwise it was all just change,
glimmers of light, faces at the window,
whispers of good intention.

From his own porch in ambiguous morning
he watches security guards
prowl the house next door
where an alarm had gone off, goes off
still, and there is no answer.

Recovery

He lives in countries now
that never knew you. Pain
falls to earth and *becomes* earth.
Wind spreads word of impending change.

All your friends have new addresses.
You think of them there in exile, steel ships
coursing in from strange lands,
leaving again for strange lands.

A cabin boy watches his hands
burn in lamplight.
Rain taps at the edge of their lives and lovers
hold one another's sex

in dry hands. The voyage is over.
Someone says: The voyage is over.

The shark fin of aloneness
heaves up against this still sky. Loss
and our hero find themselves surrounded
by a city, trees, beach, sea.

Happy Endings

After the party I unsnare each wire
with the tool provided, watch
house driveway car
fall into the sky. It's almost
morning: little dark left
to hold them back.

I think how you steered me
on your arm in there
from friend to friend
for introductions, saying
George Amy Burt Marybeth
I'd like you to meet my husband.

All these things falling
towards stars now. Overcome
with the beauty of it, you appear
at my shoulder, knowing
what I will say: that
you are my wire, I was almost gone.

Chemin

Whatever you want remains
behind; still, there are paths
you didn't follow.

You enter the afternoon for which you were looking.
There is a garden
and here you may rest:

vague thoughts of endurance
behind shut eyes.

On the lawn exhaustion
tumbles behind

your words. The small arches of the day
house you, the wind
supports you in this.

You could be part in that defeat,
that clearing.
You could surrender what you have,
refuse what is offered;
attach yourself to objects.

Just to believe that

within those branches are faces, and behind
them birds. On the line of morning.

There are places
you will not go,
words you'll never hear spoken —

another kind of sadness.

The morning is deep and filled

with freedom. Again today
we try to understand this.

A book is the death of trees

and soon we become lonely
prey to sorrow ourselves.

Our souls the coagulation
of nervous force — but not alone.

These other things
congeal: blood, milk,

the air you move against.

21

❖

The wall stands alone.
Substance, syntax
pared away; it is drained of association.
In this, one could find a language of objects.

❖

Impenetrable:
drop of ink, an orchid
in the glass beside you.

Unacknowledged:
the skin of water, flowers erupting
from it.

Unaccountable:
the vacant trees
and memory, the mocassins of sorrow.

There was repose, a pause,
not rest:

convergence and concentration,
undivided. People spoke together

in the shifting winds
that took their voices.

The wind, around its gills
insensible, insubstantial.

As the sun moves,
the center, so do you,
there at the edge of a lawn.

There is no arrival;
there is simply being there.

It is enough; it remains.

In Memory

Sometimes at night, with my coffee, thoughts,
weight settling
into the corners of the house,

you would appear
against the sky, your torn face
admitting stars: the only light there was.

Our second year: darkness
poured from the ground, rose about us.
In thin air, rising ourselves,
we huddled together for warmth,

passed whatever air remained
back and forth between us,
breathing into and out of one another.

Then I stood watching you
violated by sleep.

Towards dawn I would feel your body
stiffen, burning
in that pale flame.

You had begun to drift up into light
baring its teeth,
into betrayals of morning.

Storm that plunges on
unappeased, red candle, batter of blood
within cupped hands.

By the grace of moments
you left death behind.

Earth wells up beneath us.
Blue pours from bucket to bucket,
yellow leaps across the sky.

Moths tear at night's black flannel.

Till one night your name
flew out of the mouths of the dead.

Lying beside you then, I learned
what bodies are for:

you with your wing
of death, your degree.

Palely in twilight, the candle
flutters about its memory
of moths.

Evening has gone home to fix dinner
for its children, and you are alone.

O comforting darkness:
do not forget us, do not leave us
here waiting.

At last, past our windows,
the storm gives itself to the night.

In water standing on roofs
across the street, all the city's lights
melt into a single light.

O roofs and forgiveness
in the shuddering dawn.

Boston

A ship comes into harbor,
rain seeking gutters
at the edge of the roof.

In the aquarium, lungfish
close their eyes.

Two crabs, alone in zinc
and bodies, mimic
the end of all our loves.

Yellow

I'm thinking how he came
to us late one afternoon, loping over the fence
with a gap like a smile in his belly, broken
and proud. But the hole in him
closed and he stayed, returning here
even at the end, to our front porch.

I found him when I came
home from work. My stethoscope revealed
an empty lung, the other filled
with blood. He could scarcely
lift his head. His skull appeared to be
pushed in at the back, elongated,
like the skulls of prehistory
horses: already his body was settling.

The two of us existed by code, I suppose,
tolerating one another. The yard was his;
I did not invade it. But he moves into
the green stretch of my mind now, and I cannot
move away from him. I think he may have deserved
that final struggle.

I'm thinking, too, as I do so often
now, about the space she left me
to reconstruct a life. Yellow came and went,
his own wandering ancient world,
revolving out into the dark and back
from the small simple bright of our yard.
I wouldn't have been much. How many times
did I see him take on cats twice his size
and drive them from the yard?
And when the world shrank
at last from open fields and free
lots, shrank to a single hot seed
of pain, the last big cat, he fixed it
with his eyes and would not let go.

He died in the afternoon while I slept.
In our back yard new kittens move
towards games with grasshoppers and I watch,
admiring the ancient grace in every quick
motion, these awkward beginnings, the violent calm
circling even now above their heads.

Beauty

There in the garden where
she burns among flowers

Having abandoned
this room, these solid walls

A part of her remains here
Even from escape she slips away

And so I sit
watching her burn among the flowers

Mouth open, red hair blazing

Country Music

He appears
in the city. This is amazing.
Drunk of course (he can't remember
the letter he sent
last week) and raging. Sorry
he hasn't seen her lately. Looking
for her now — but she's gone.

Crops crumble back
down their stalks. Men in fields
(men with hammers, fences down)
walk large in the dusk. With
the shadows of hammers
they beat at the shadows of fences.
Gravel is under their heels.

Jazz

Curls of smoke from the city
surround his eyes: the pits
of pearl-gray pears.

On the hill up here above it
there's little more to say;
David's scarf beats in the wind,

a limp tongue attempting speech.
Our eyes fall like circling birds,
water in a drain, to the scene below.

Yoked to the city's ruin, he'll find
his own in cool departures, separate customs,

eyes moving to new places like twin hammers,
resonant, sustaining.

What Pavese Said

Embrace my loneliness.
Don't ask me to leave it.

Though you can ask anything of me,
there are things you cannot ask.

In time I will tell you
more, always more.

When I lie beside you
in blinding night,

I know the future
of our love, and all things.

In the Realm

(for Kierkegaard)

In the end, it's said, inward
clarity and peace came over him.
Doubt, his daily companion, left him
for someone else.

All of it came back to him there
on the street, everything
he had exiled from life and mind.

The life of the spirit moves upwards
in abrupt stages; the life of the mind
hovers, returns.

Postmen said: Søren, here is the stamp
you asked for. It will forward you
into faith, into the Absolute.
Momentum will overcome you.

To a man they shuffled feet
and stuttered. This
will be our secret, they all said.

For Guillevic

Roses, meadows, open
to us: a lesson of objects.

One moves among them
as through rooms
of half-remembered faces.

The cry of the iris
returns from the woods,
where it was lost.

Bushes assemble
under an oak in moonlight.

Even in the city
we hear this, approaching dawn,
and awaken.

Dawn

(à Yves Bonnefoy)

I have seen you, Dawn, at the pane of my window; an eye in the corner, a swift movement and the early evening.

I have seen you in the afternoon garden. One hand to your breast where you burned among flowers, beneath this solitary room.

I have seen you in flight from bees that swept about you there, aware too late of their wings' intent, your mouth open to whisper *Les papillons! les papillons!*

I have seen you at the point of despair, a door, a gate, looking back. And your eyes.

I have seen you lying beneath the sky's regard, arms stretched out, Dawn, wide and free as a fence.

Your body open, that nothing would enter.

Event

They are moving the city again. For the third time this
year men arrive in their trucks and brown trousers, smiling.
They drive their vehicles wildly like Dodg'em Cars among,
into, against the buildings. Walls, windows, doors fall into
the backs of the trucks and the trucks begin to move away,
out of the city; to take them somewhere else. The remains
are washed away by torrential rains, which follow.

Old Poems

We pass on the street
and do not recognize one another.
We sit side by side at a bar
talking for hours, saying nothing.
You want a refill, hon? asks
the waitress in her pocket-sprung apron.
Beautiful day, this old poem of mine
tells me as we walk by the river.
Out on a wide belt of water
boats eclipse one another.
I have no idea
what he's talking about.

Meeting Myself

Young man that I was,
what can I say to you?
We meet at a party, stand together
near a sofa, hemmed in by other lives,

men who crawl through the city
in the black carapaces of cars,
women who watch with red lips
from doors and second-floor windows.

You were so serious, young man —
I remember. As Thoreau said
of Emerson: there was a fire in your mind
burning cord after cord of wood,

the cord of What I Believe,
the cord of How We Come To Be,
the cord of The Future,
the cord of Everything Else.

Perhaps even now when women stand
in windows and doorways
and look out across the city —
perhaps it's those flames they watch for.

When the black cars stop before them
and they bend to touch doors
lightly, the steel is hot.
It burns the hands of their children.

How It Started

One morning in 1968 on my way for coffee
at 7 A.M. I passed myself on the street.
I was standing at a bus stop
looking a little lost, wearing
a sweatshirt the color of mustard,
cut-offs, run-over mocassins.

Excuse me, one of us said, but do you have
the time? I could smell night's darkness on me,
a skein of sweat, detergent and fresh air
in the sheets, last night's woman.

No watch, one of us said. No watch,
no dollar for the ticket, no life.
Not much ambition either, come
to think of it. How about you?

One of us shrugged. One of us
held out a struck match, though
the other had stopped smoking. Know
just how you feel, he said.

Special Effects

This is what I did not expect.
A skeleton opens the trailer door,
walks in and sits on the couch by me.
In an effort to be up-to-date
it wears a baseball cap with the bill
turned to the back.
I pass the bowl of popcorn across to it,
but it refuses with a wave of its hand.
Knucklebones crack.
We watch The Rockford Files together
a while. I haven't seen this one before,
the skeleton says.

So how's it been going, Son? it says
when the commercials come on.
I never meant to put off coming round
this long, you know.
For a moment its attention is taken
by a set of disembodied talking teeth
on the screen. Amazing what they can do
these days. The show comes back on,
Jim and his father grousing as usual,
and we watch. Looking from screen to window,
the skeleton says, Going to rain soon,
all my joints ache: a sure sign.

Some Years into It

I almost have it. I could pass now
in all but the most discerning
company. You would walk through
the room, though. And when I cried out,
when the proper words tripped on my tongue and fell,
they would know
I am not what we all pretend to be.

I almost have it now, the shape
of this heart
like a hive of bees in my two hands,
this bladder, this bag of other bags
like a pot I go on forming
as I turn towards you, turning it
in my hands.

All our other, older selves
look on, heels hooked in the fence slats,
where they've got it right. And whatever
I've worked so hard at carrying to you
across this green floor, through this crowd,
in the moment I arrive smiling
is never there.

Last Best Friend

(for Lee Goerner)

My name is Death: the last best friend am I.
— Robert Southey

1.

On Sunday morning, bright and two weeks
after the flood, the phone rings,
shouldering its way in
between breakfast and a third cup of tea.
With knowledge that you've died,
cracks between planks
in the floor of the world broaden.

Out there, scored to the whine
of a blue kettle, people and cars
shrug themselves upward, forward, into day.
Faces of women drift across windows. Their bodies
step into the frames of open doorways,
aslant there like books on half-filled shelves,
feet set square on the floor of the world.

Once we believed these tides of literature
would bear us up, into some other place — how?
You with two bad legs, my own double-edged life,
both atilt, planes banking sideways
with stopped engines, stop-time, into sea.
This time at least you don't go on circling, Lee,
waiting for clearance.

43

This time there'll be no happy ending,
no handful of survivors clinging to the wreckage,
telling how they learned to fill their bellies
with batting from seat cushions,
how at first they lived off the bodies
of fellow passengers, later
off the fleshy parts of their own hands.

2.

Form rarely saves anything but itself.
Its statues and memorials aren't ours. Nor
(having come to a time when voids in our life,
what isn't there, was never there,
is there no longer, define those lives
precisely) should we find form
near so fetching as formerly.

Before the heart's cables snap,
we might have said then as New York
or French Quarter streets swept beneath us
and we made our way on shaky new sea legs
back to whatever rooms awaited us,
their cloisters and crow's nests, holds
stacked with boxes.

Memory, too, like silvered envelopes
of the coffee you never drank,
though our wives and myself (back at the hotel
off Canal, you nursed ailing feet)
willowed over the dark fires of cups
to the sound of Thirties swing through the window
and boat horns from the river.

Black children with bottle caps
on their shoes for taps awaited us in doorways.
All music and language is the same: pitch,
duration, attack. Gray-green ships
mute and heavy as tanks
moved on the river. Everything comes down
to salvage, Lee — including our lives.

We'd turned ourselves into creatures
of imagination, pinning up on the horizon
quotes we could live by,
cartoons, titles, letters from friends
who hand-drew at the top of the page
in lieu of letterhead or heading
harpies with billowing, pillowy breasts.

3.

Like America itself, I suppose,
our lives were anthologies, private museums.
Here, large as a car,
is the drill we used to dredge silver
from reluctant ground, here recreations
(for no one remembers them now)
of the songs we hummed as we worked.
On benches bolted into cement we sat
watching the river comb through itself,
washing up at land's foot whatever was foreign.
Like memory those benches were shelves
where long ago feelings had been rendered down, put up,
as mere sensation — pleasure or pain;
form at its best, preserves.

You were right, Lee: hands burned like candles
at the altars of dead gods. We embraced
bare forms, whispers of Platonic ghosts,
the hollowed-out cheeks of catechism —
as though it took a mess of shadows for its meat —
looking wisely back and forward, savoring this stew
of things left over.

No one saw where our gestures ended,
quick movements in the corners
of rooms, furtive eclipses at the very edge of light:
shadows, volumes. Are any of us, ever,
anything more? Adding up all the columns
on this Easter morning one year later, still
I tally every one to zero — where you live now.

Katherine has brought candy eggs. In the hotel lobby
off St. Charles and Canal she opens her hand face down:
now they are ours. While on this *other* Easter
we all — Katherine, Karyn, myself, all
your soundless friends, Lee, this yearlong later —
hunt memory, streets and lives of the past
for presents you've left behind.

Among the Missing

Nailed to the chair
by old songs, my hands still
on this purring machine.

A word almost forms before me, at the last minute
turns its face away, folds its tent
and fades without comment.
Its lawyer arrives in grey pinstripes.

The spirit's been known to escape in such crowds,
running off with a deep scream
clutching its bag of hamburgers
into the press of bodies and distance.

The reporter says: I came upon him in Akron
eating the sky. He had a knife in one hand,
a jar of relish, a mouthful.
Put that down, you fool, you don't know
what you're doing, I told him.
You don't know what might happen.

Accused of pretense, I deliver my case
and rest. The edges of those days
flash like blades, quick, in the sun.
Leather dries and tightens over the pulse,
into flesh. I did not know the sun here
was so unforgiving: I believed

they would tell us, not die,
tongues black and swollen like hanged men's.

Something inside goes away now,
out over the grazing heads of the houses
in just a slight wind,
and I watch — out across the river,

old thoughts no longer useful.
I admire lizards green like copper
in the firebead. They arc and falter,
rest on their ribs in the froth of leaves.

Tony, we have other wives and lives.
Different rivers flow through us now.
Make room, among regret's troops,
for new recruits; the sky fans
out from our shoulders, connecting them.
We are white bats keening at unseen presence.

Such freedom persists in these ranks,
the sick remain so much more interesting. But fancy
seldom bags what it starts to flight,
and we cull from among the damaged and infirm perhaps

a plateful, a trophy.
These grounds, we should know, are posted.

On small tables parading our pitiful rages
till the spring winds down. Drums halt, characters topple.
And we are blank as potatoes.
We plead amendments, feel that quiet menace
seeping in at the far edge of lives.
Push our heads free of the ground to talk.

Light pours from the window
as the sun falls.

The rain was too deadly then,
bloated bellies of clouds like grey frogs
above us; between cities
we were the legs of locusts whirling.
The rage of Caliban, I suppose, or something of it:
mirrors should be kinder.

But his glass won't contain us now.
In the heart of this country with its heady beer we declaim
Columbus the perfect poet.
His taste for the exotic and long trips,

getting lost, naming his craft for women.
Poets rarely go where they intend either:
the craft itself wanders.
Our lives sink into such connections.

Soon there'll be nothing left, Tony. Nothing
but light moving out endlessly into far galaxies
with its cardboard suitcase and no passport.

The flood waters lug back. Someone invents
the blues, newspapers, a guitar. Recording contracts!
Things begin to move very quickly at this point.
The streets of New York were always a mystery to me.

So were Iowa's.
I used to imagine camels clopping among the hills there,
stores of munitions in Amish cellars
beside preserves and mushrooms. The mind
will not let things go; it pays that price.
Windmills spun fitfully across their land,

dividing the earth's breath into manageable portions.
Now in Texas those fields drawl around me again
and a similar harvest prepares.
We cut ourselves loose from so much.

Days go on muttering into afternoon, some of their words
so long that people chime in, just to get them said,

to get that much done at least.
Strings peel from your guitar one by one in the closet.
A case might be made, I think, for abuse, putting it
with foster parents for a time;

this certainly needs looking into.
Please complete the enclosed forms and return them.

A cat we had, a male
that followed my daughter home one day, adopted
a sick kitten spurned by its mother, lay beside it
day and night in the cardboard box. Now it will not eat
and cannot breathe. I have been trying all night
to think of something that doesn't mean more than
    it should.

I hear my daughter's breath in the next room
as I write, a small dry tide.

Spume of unspent days, the coxswain's call
as we round the cape into morning. Costly
delays then as documents are forged, and reinforcements
arrive at the crusades too bloody damned tired to care.

They live on air. On lichen scraped from smooth
    stones, moss
from the bends of trees. They grow close to the earth.
Its own breath passes through them, fogs the mirror.
No question now of propriety, precedent.

But of a sudden they swoon. Abulia
is the new patron; they cannot choose. Stand in streams
casting their eyes about them. This is faith
of a kind; it ticks in them like a tapeworm.

Earth tears away from them.
Their teeth harden.

We'd best have done with conventions
of language, sustain interest and effect
otherwise, Tony. Once you returned to me poems
    Byronically
cast from the balcony minutes before.
Things are always lugging back up onto the shore like that.
You learn to watch your feet when you walk.

Particle theory, the behavior of worms.
It all seems so clear some mornings.
But the day dogs on and darkens; dark shapes
cross the fields to beckoning trees

hung with Spanish moss, clung to
by kudzu. We turn into unfamiliar streets,

poets of the crackerbarrel and marzipan,
wrapped in starchy sheets, beating at hollow logs.
Often we amaze ourselves and others throw coins.
The trip back is always much quicker.

You can't play much horn when your teeth fall out,
but Bunk still hits all the joints, hoping
for a chance to blow some. Mostly soul, old progressions,
he can slip right into the middle of that, with those kids.

Choking down oatmeal we cross the field. Eat
sugar cane at the open market; milk in our coffee
at the Café du Monde. Fill watermelons with gin.
Filing away letters of intent, self-depositions.

Ah — the journey then. Tracks not in as good
repair, I think, as before. And service appalling.
A group of detectives inhabits the next car but one,
some sort of convention as I understand. We pass repeatedly
by men in fur hats and leggings at the side of the road.
A dozen small towns hunch their backs at us and turn away.

We sit in the bus's butt unwrapping ham sandwiches
that cost a buck and slid out of machines
like newspapers which is pretty much the way they taste too.
Volleys of enemy fire furrow the road around us.

Memory comes clipping back into camp
with its blackened face, stuttering and staring ahead.
You know how that is.

Volition wraps itself in wind,
whips at my window: Don't deny my name.
Sister Kate shimmies on the levee with a couple
of horny oboe players driving Chevies. Poor mom. I hope
you don't mind my writing you on this hotel stationery;
what's a little bad taste between friends.

Tony, I'm coming more and more to realize
it's not strength that matters but endurance,
and mud has us all beat. The earth doesn't need
anything new: does well enough with what it has.

The fact that style's essentially an act of faith
probably has something to do with the poverty of style now.

And really *all* streets are a mystery to me,
implying arrivals, corners, clear demarcation.
The wind is not like that, memory is not like that.
Nor the hemp collar drawing tighter,

the tiny stacks of words that will put you away.
They drop us by copter into the middle of the swamp
where for the next forty years we will raise potatoes
and squash. The commandant gives a speech
saying no one's ever escaped from here
and grinning like a gator himself. You can almost sense

credits (long delay is now stylish) rolling up over
the assembled faces, a single shade for all those windows.

Naturally we escape, riding the subway to safety,
all we own carried with us in shopping bags.
A banjo player in Jackson Square does a medley
of *Swanee River, We Shall Overcome* and Vivaldi.

He wears sandals and jeans, greying hair gathered
beneath a bandana, uses the banjo as a cane
as he rocks back out onto the street. His eyes have
the dull sheen of a thing that accepts its place in history.

The young men in their suits are blue-eyed and wild.
The sky moves through them like a razor.

The women are stern and children drop
from their limbs like ripe apples.

They learn to read following fingers along
lists of concerts and art exhibits. Their chests
burn with knowledge. It beats within them,
finds its way finally to their throats.
They make beautiful sounds. And we starve,
gorged on potatoes, rice, squash, melon.

We are old friends, my friend, this quiet
dolour and I. Indolence is in me, a child,
a roomer who will not pay his way but resists
eviction. Ambition kills, nothing else. Be safe.

When the lesson is over we fold our books
if we have books, pack away the instruments,
approach the quotidian — do you remember?

A frightening moment, even with the road signs,
these constant maps. We will go too far;
our penetration will prove inadequate;

we will not understand it after all.
Hunger is so great and there is so little food.

Sunlight climbs the wall. So much depends
on the donkeys of memory. Morning washes over us.
This story comes to me, Tony: That a child
passes through the walls of a road
across centuries and clouds. Every few moments
he stops at the edge of the road

and cries, then goes on. What else
can the child do, he knows nothing of any of this.
What does a child know of the sky.

In his hand a glass flower tries to hold
the last light of the sun, the very last light of the sun.

P.S.

See me, riding out
crosslegged from an Arkansas fog-
farm; initial impact
ending, twenty years later, in a bad
back, cracked health, weak
arms.

    My father a short man
with the face of an Indian. Places
like Los Alamos, Oak Ridge; a welder,
fusing the seams of shards later
put (and without his ever knowing) into
the bomb: Bang. And Daddy
comes home.

    My mother like dozens,
hundreds of others told
to have no more children; but
has one, me after seven years,
and her nerves jangling still, scraped
on the ends with every
move I make; a canteloupe slice,
a scooped-out woman.

    My brother John, round
face at the edge of my bed, collaborations
of parental persuasion. Now a man too,
like the bowl of a pipe. A philosopher,
teacher; wife and two daughters
in far-off Pittsburgh.

❖

                    And
I grew up and the fig trees
in the backyard
stopped.

                    Once when I was five
I fell from one (small enough
to climb in a fig tree!) and
couldn't breathe
for what seemed hours. When you broke
the figs off, a few drops
of strange stiff milk
came out from the stem; honeysuckle
too, like that, a thin drop of
something like nectar. And grapes —
there were grapes, for a few
years. My brother and I, sitting
in the big swing made
from a door and cables, lobbing
one another with the seeds.

                    Now
down all the corridor nautilus years,
myself with a wife and son: London.

❖

New Orleans, and a friendly bird
at the zoo in Audubon Park.

                              Years ago
they buried an elephant on top
of the ground here; a hill,
that the children
play on. I studied Chaucer
in the afternoon, entered in
plays, read Melville and Hawthorne
for the first time. It was a time for firsts,
and you broke
into those forms like a nail
into cork: Jane.

So we climbed up a trellis
of rooms;
and in one of those rooms
(a room with the windows turned
inside; an old sheepskin moulding
in the tub; smoked cheese,
copies of Baudelaire, chalk
drawings) I
came into you with all the
simple violence
by which, weeks before, you
had entered my life. Mardi Gras
beads chattered on the doorknobs.

Then with luggage (and you
like a piece of luggage) to Iowa,
with the birds behind us. Till
one afternoon you felt
the strings tightening.

When Dylan was born
I was downstairs reading Pound.
I had missed an interview
with Dali; I ate three hamburgers
in celebration; my term paper on
little magazines was late.

Signals we are set here
to read. Conceivably. Now,
from far-off legendary Arkansas you write
that strange little tumors are growing
in the walls of your stomach;
that Dylan's bowel movements are
regular, he is doing well with sentences;
that my brother is coming
to visit and would like to see me; that (P.S.)
you enjoy misspelling and singing.

Preparing for the Hurricane

Behind locked shutters we squat
like cave-age folk, white eyes rolling,
with our stack of books, candles,
canned food, new plastic trashcan
filled with water.

Squirrels that each morning and afternoon
climb the banana trees in our back yard
and clutter the patio with shreds
of leaves and dark red bloom, now cling,
confused, beneath the eaves.

Wind, after all, is a kind of speech,
and when it comes, even these
taped windows will chatter. And so
we crouch here remembering water,
our pure idea of it, all our pure ideas.

Living with You

Another year and the ground
pulls harder,

the heart
on its intricate stalk succumbs again

to your hair, your breath and voice.

A tree
grows, and the world grows

smaller. A pan on the stove,
boiling too much water,

raises the level of entropy in the world.

Asking for Help

David, I've fallen
in love again. (I know,
at my age I should know
better; but I didn't mean to.)

Soon the phone
will ring, she'll ask me over.
Last night we stood at the door
stunned by our feelings

like teenagers, running tongues
into mouths and hands under clothes.
I couldn't sleep.
All day I have watched the clock

as though suspecting it of theft.
In morning sunlight I was
weightless, pure. I cannot forget
the feel of her rib under my hand,

her lean fingers. Do we ever recover
from this terrible ache, David,
from these words wanting eternally
to be born in us? Must we know

all our lives this wanting,
these hollows? I hope
you can tell me, David,
there with your new wife.

To a Friend with Good Counsel

I add your advice to that of Aristophanes
and look out for holes beneath my feet.
But friend, you know that advice is but
for the giving, to be got rid of. Unlike
these women we lay alongside.

They are as strange as we are, and deeper.
We hold them to us, searching
for salvation between their legs, or
(you would chide me) in mere art.
You want me out of their dark and repetitions.

O my friend, for your counsel I love you,
but loved you already, and have loved
your words at least as long.
So many years I did not write.
So many years I did not live.

Yet even as a child I knew this world
of dentists and executions to be hopelessly
exotic. That I could not live in this world,
only beside it. In fanciful masks I will visit,
send postcards. I have your address.

We've known other wives, and the old
songs die within us. I tell you
there will be only a few to carry on, that
we will never be loved again as we have been.
Yes, David: the air at world's edge is thin.

I see them tumbling over horizons, all
those future poets thin as cypress,
their saucer-big eyes turning in air,
casting about in the fall for good advice, help,
hard words, the hopeful shores of women.

Santa Fe

Onstage, in what critics will call
a brilliant metaphor of solitude, a man
stands turning with mouth open.
He starts to speak, realizes there is
no audience, turns again. Another,
playing Darkness, comes to a sudden stop
at the edge of the stage and
begins to grow larger.

Moons tumble up there
among the old world's spars and columns,
and stories lie down in vacant lots
around us. All night long
wind in the chimes outside, in its clipped,
nearly-familiar voice, says over and over
I'd like you to meet,
I'd like you to meet . . .

From our cave hanging in air
like a dark sun, we look out over these plains
where day in animal skins
with its crooked spear of language
hunts food, and women left behind
watch dampness on the cave's wall sketch out
the idea of fire, loneliness,
art shows, daily newspapers.

We flew back for a weekend
into the world of wood, memories
packhorsed beneath dark mountains,
bright adobe. There
at midnight, with snow gathering in those
mountains, with the pulse of music coming up
from below, you found sky and cried,
leaning into me like a ladder.

Writing at Night

Facing again the limitless well
of words into which round periods
expire without sound.

In moonlight outside, pursuing
their own transformations, garbage bags
take on fantastic, animate forms.

I watch them graze and preen.
In the morning they'll be gone.
Poems will have taken their place.

So the trees again refuse
to be only trees. And of time, still
we see only its back, hurrying away.

I watch these black bags choose mates
and breed in the moonlight, tossing
their small heads, lumpy bodies

dumb with joy as they couple
in the moonlight; watch how they fall back
exhausted then, and move no more.

In My Solitude

(for Duke Ellington)

Another morning:
with hands capable
of anything
I will touch you,

body turning
like a river in my mind.

O the feet traveling in pairs
on the road beyond
my window.

O your hands
at the rim of the world prying
apart my solitude.

Trying to Surface

One falls asleep, and the other lies
in the litter of his history, looking out
at a pale moon, trying to surface.

As a child you built houses
for frogs, drawing furniture and rooms
inside cardboard boxes:

you loved them. But shut in those
houses they died, dry skins
waiting for you come morning.

I trace the branch of veins
in one breast with a finger, wait
for your silent terror to subside.

Words have carried us deep
into morning and marooned
us here, your pale body pure

as mist rising from the pond outside.
Under this unimagined moon,
dipping branches bear the weight

of our losses. I think:
still water, another woman, same hands
at the clock. Tonight

you will not talk to me, and silence
gathers like mist, settles between us
on this bed narrow as a grave.

Because of this at this moment I know
something of the future, how it will
give itself to us slowly, its reticence.

Coalgate

Your life grows smaller
and smaller behind you.
Eyes set for unexpected curves,
falling rock, animals,
you speed through the hall past me.

Reading, I hear beneath us
the slap of old tires that may not make it,
the lug of our engine as we head
into foothills, feel
the pull of ground at my chest.

Bright rooms come up around us.
Over coffee we remember what it was like:
folding our lives into cars, road breaking
over our bow, how we go on arriving.
And lean again into these sudden turns.

Halfway House

Home for a weekend, she rises
into the rare air
of afternoon sleeping,
tongues of terror lapping at her
as Gilligan washes over.

A man with missing teeth attempts
to whistle. She circles
with hawks above a valley
where severed hands graze,
clutching at honeysuckle and iris.

When she is gone again,
her shoes go on walking towards him
across the floor.

Love Poem

"It's a complex fate, to be an American."
—Henry James

I traveled to far countries and learned to speak of the weather. But when I returned they all spoke of art.

Undaunted I studied bowling, accordion, the stock market: I would be there waiting, on the long low plane of the commonplace, when they returned. But they left for Europe.

I enrolled in jazz, American studies, beginning football. My professors spoke French.

Only you now to define and surround me. Watching the others roll away in their crocodile boats, feeling behind me the encroachment of black American forests.

Piano Poem

In the dark alley where poems grow,
hunching their shoulders
for more space and weeping
over stories read in newspapers
that blow by them there on windy days,

there are also pianos. The pianos
are restless, bothered; they do not sleep well,
and rolling about in the night, unwittingly
kill dozens of poems to whom they dedicate
in the morning, glittering Chopin etudes.

Celebration

So little left of you
in this large room
filled with the empty logic
of objects. They assume
position from your leaving.

The others watch me glide
from wall to wall, room
to room, on this smooth surface
you've left
behind. They laugh.

The news not good today,
but "positive." Nothing in the post;
your movements, gestures,
dragged down from the sky
like dull heavy birds.

Tablets, then,
for the daily morning tongue,
a departure,
so little left, a little
blood on the sheets.

The Surrealist's Vacation

Beneath this sun
putting on and taking off
its yellow hat

in Bermudas and tan shirt he strides
doggedly into the center of the flower

where time's bee
has new itineraries for him,

irrevocable visas, books of memories,
letters home.

Fair Weather

Today
I erect
hurricanes.

Direct earthquakes to your house.
Handle the winds, make a secret sign
to the sun and send rain
back up to hide in your windows.

Your crops will steam on the stem
until you listen.
The eyes of your cattle
will burn, turn red and run down

into their mouths; towns disappear
as the sea returns like Faust
to its ancient mansions —
until you listen.

Then to a few (never you)
I'll allow
redemption, like a candle.

New York at 3 A.M.

Lost
in the middle distance, waving
Clubs of silence passed through
her hands

And I,
riding towards her
This absurd awkward ostrich
Sand in its clubbed toes

Crying
Wait! Wait! Water
at her knees

Love

The words this fire
balances
on its many tongues.

Need, that gray
biscuit hard as
the spine's own wafers.

Hands that hold
cloth ladders, a nest
of red bowls.

To wake *with*.
To know the name
of morning.

Rain

(for Denis Roche)

I'll have the rain
In my pockets, eyes
In the torn clouds

The clouded
Tears
Formed of lumber

And the sea returns, a ghost
In the well

In the lumbering clouds
The torn leaves
Leave

Earthfish

New York Poems

He or the other. This room
the world
and a world beyond.

You came down
and turned on the light
in the room where I work. I was writing
A bird flies
A leaf falls
A branch holds down the sun.

The turtle has lived
a week in the teacup now
rimmed with sugar and flies.

Making tea — just
as the water blossoms.

From your room on Riverside Drive you watch
as old lovers float away
from you and out over New Jersey,
change of address cards tucked
in their pockets.

Your answers come
walking out of cold
subways at night,
alone in plastic raincoats.

"What do you want from me,
no, what do you really want."

Outside, cars drive
into the East River, lining up
politely
to wait their turn.

Tom left with his blue tea service
yesterday, in his red patent leather
shoes, across the white snow.

Planes are arriving from London
so fast
that men on the field waving them in
have got their arms tangled together
into knots.

On each of those planes
you sit
with knees crossed inside your new trousersuit
sipping tea and smiling.

I feel like singing, he said.
Because she threw a shoe at me
on her way away,
I feel like singing.

We've seen the sun
rip through ribbons into morning,
a man torn to shreds by wind
on the street one afternoon,
bullets that wandered through Manhattan
till they found the right man.

Jagged line of these buildings
against the sky, as though
something has been torn away there.

I begin to catalog what you've left behind:
drawings, mirror, winter, a solitary shoe.
Morning spreads across the sky,

a yellow burn. First cloud of coffee,
almost red, rolling out into clear water.

You enter the room. A shelf of manuscripts,
windows, New York behind me.
I am larger than you remember.

You move towards me now. Furniture,
lamps resolve into photographs.
You are standing still.

My hand disappears at the corner
of the canvas. Your body
is hardly there, an ill-defined
buttock, parts of legs. While I

loom above you, a physicality
of emaciated torso, impossible legs
bent double, dark face. My other arm,
with its hand, does not appear.

❖

Fog moves along the bottom
of the window, orange
against park lamps outside.

I turn on the lights and forget
why I've come: caught here, naked,
with the mouthful of air I carried between rooms.

Two Scenes from the Revolution

1.

Robespierre does not know that the wolf wants only to talk. *Wait*, he says, *I am but an agent of the people; it is they whom you must eat.*

What of this new government? the wolf asks.

There is no government, only the people.

The people will that I should eat you, the wolf says.

But that, surely, is only because they are misguided; they do not have the facts.

2.

Danton's head, as it rolls from the guillotine, continues speaking.

It is much more complicated than we believed, gentlemen.

As the executioner lifts the head for display: *I thank you for your support.*

We will speak together again. Now I must think about all that has happened.

For a long time the head is silent.

News of the Absolute

"There is only one real
tree, copied over and over inside you
and without,
to produce these others."

Plato and Heraclitus are having lunch.
Plato orders cheese and fruit;
Heraclitus keeps changing his mind
and finally does without.

Over coffee they look up
and see Hegel. He brings fresh news
of the absolute. Reality, he says,
is bullish on today's market.

Principles of Aesthetics

There are more obscure points
to be made, but I'm not sure
we have time.

Words have no knowledge;
only our fear
knows the names of things.

Remember: real warts
on imaginary frogs.

If truth has lawyers,
or beauty, we're all dead.

As we grow old, we grow
eyes in the backs of our heads
to see behind us, useless eyes.

Colons hold us; with periods
we begin our descent to life.

In the shopping mall, improbably,
a bird flies to your shoulder.

The sound of rain
gathering on flat roofs. Insomnia,
an old friend, collects me from sleep.

Grammars

1.

Evening As a
Reflexive Verb

Within themselves hands rest
as in the lowering forest
evening is prepared.

Here will be a gathering,
as of growth so slow
it goes unnoticed.

When the tall stalks
are cut down
at last, we are there.

2.

Imperatives

In my mirror it's the sea
today, suddenly grown
unafraid of the crowd.

Keeps company
only with proud sky, with
insects that huddle

in earth's warm palm
and are never seen. This water
a blue wound, wanting.

It will take your face
away to Greece, Istanbul.
You must speak to it.

3.

Declensions
of Memory

There is nothing you can take
with you of this day, nothing
but its ashen light perhaps.

Your hands rise
as though expecting welcome
from the sky.

You must learn
the words that bring great sorrow,
healthy children, rain.

In your eyes will dwell,
one after another,
a thousand forgotten worlds.

Borders

At the border shall evening
stop to show papers;
will it be admitted?

The storm moves
hesitantly
towards that far land.

At the instant
it crosses, the word
changes itself.

For a moment, looking
down, a sparrow pauses.
Wolves follow
the line of the border.

There is trouble: wind
has again forgotten its passport.

Border, do you love
your two parents?

Apostrophe

The dead are so private,
that's the thing.

I have wound myself in bleached sheets,
laid for days under a dripping pipe
in the cellar, and still
I don't know them.

At night I stack pillows
above my head and open my ears
to the black oil about me.

A democrat, I will not abide
this aristocracy. Marxist,
I decry such privileged possession.

Surely reason establishes death
as the highest form of being.

And they never answer my letters.

Animist

The words of the dead
I have learned to live with.

Always they are coming out
of my pockets, my mouth.

In my hand I carry
their dark bodies

about the world. This
is the use they have of me.

Saturdays

It will be good, heading into the sunset when this is all over.

We, fool and coward, have learned trust as the bullets finally tired and fell around us.

You tell me of your childhood back east, how the old man was always drunk.

The pretty young schoolmarm falls in love with an atheist.

Sentient mud has just done in Godzilla.

Attack of Literature

To be so weary of what
we steer by. I fear open doors, the voices
of young girls and their strong legs.

At night the radio and I whisper
unspeakable things to one another —
books no longer console me.

On a day like this, poetry will return,
slamming its legs down on our cities,
its terrible voice causing the earth

to tremble as it looks into the sky,
vague memories of lost worlds
rolling in its huge, hollow bones.

Evolutions of the Day

That sound you just heard was
the day slamming its doors. Dear Sir: Please return
the free sample we sent; we regret to inform you
that your credit is ruined.
And I had thought it was life that would find me
as I sat here and waited.

There's always something to bring back.
Where shall we put Europe today?
Broken eggs are delivered in the morning post,
Dear Sir, Your subscription has expired.
When you came here all you wanted was to leave
all that, and have kind eyes.

There is a sense of returning,
of the weight of doors. In the next room, or the next,
she waits. The window becomes her face.
When you open her shirt
moths fly out; and her stomach
is filled with the yellow sunlight she breathed.

I was getting old, and the night
remained, I did not know what to do.
She went on talking.
A telephone rang in the cottonfield.
How's the crop this year? On the beach a crab
puts up an arm between the water and its eyes.

Twilight

Somehow tonight these insects gather up all the world's sounds. In rising circles all around us they sing and chitter. Out of their bodies unfold ancient dramas in which we had no part. Then a silence falls. As though they said: Now tell us yours, we are listening.

Newspapers

You'd bring them to me
Hidden at the bottom of your purse
Like us they were restless there
Their answers brief

I opened them inside mornings
Filled with my fingers

Waking in the afternoons we watched
Heads down they pulled themselves
Across the carpet towards sunlight
Weeping

Sorrow

That the mind might lie down
with what it has.

All night the beast
beat at the walls of its room
as I lay forgetting you.

Regret will not have my mind
in the same room with it.

New Regime

We've reached a decision
There will be no more Sundays
The Commissioner agrees

Already we have formed
A committee to investigate
This curious and alarming loss

A Complete History

Ocean would tell you, sky would tell you.
But they are busy now, holding off
infidels who have learned to walk
and the secrets of their locks.

At night you hear them, their arrows
whistling through the dark as they practice
scales with only three tones. In their dark suits
we do not see them until they are beside us.

In the final year they begin to teach us
what we have forgotten. In my son's eyes I see
new knowledge: how the hawk falls effortlessly
into sky, how the sparrow waits there.

For Mandelstam

The silent forest gathers
to the falling branch. Fallen,
it is no longer of the tree.
Nor is it a part of the earth,
for it remembers sky.

Perhaps because the forest
listens still, something else
will occur, something miraculous,
a transformation, a ransom.

In the silence and gray deeps
of the world, memory
is revised. You had forgotten
the word you wanted to say;

now even the wanting is gone,
fallen quick as stone, as this
gray sky itself, itself now
a part of your silence.

Four Jazz Choruses

1.

Because the slave could not say what he meant
he said another thing. You know
how it is: one thing leads to another.
Soon he was saying all sorts
of things he didn't mean.

2.

We took his music (that's how it was meant
to be) but he didn't tell us the secret,
what he'd *really* meant by it. Meantime,
it was shuffling off to Chicago.

3.

Jazz floated up the river like a crocodile.
In New Orleans everyone ate oysters.
Bad notes were "clams."

4.

The horn's choked note rises from a dark club,
goes out over the city's long plain,
is there like air, never settles.

When I Had My Own Place

So cold up there we burned
your passport page by page,
an old credit card, papers with lists
of things to do on them.

So afraid there in that room
I said come downstairs
with me and we grilled
kebabs on wire hangers.

Ate in the corner by the furnace with
the door open and hangers inside.
I showed you my collection, told you
how I hid when anyone came down there.

Sometimes I'd bang on pipes
at night. You understood, that was just
another language, and you liked my chairs
without seats, my boxes of old records.

It was a cold February, with a cold
March still to come. The old house
shivered. Leaving,
you asked when you might come again.

Eft

(for Roger Zelazny)

The little marine who
among the fronds and dry pebbles
once too often held back

the pod of fish and toothless
turtles from his mate now lies

in the white square of a kitchen tile.
It was a lie: he could not
survive the fire. His soft skin

and ambitious gills have
killed him. He is contained, conceived,
in this defeat. As always,

the feeling now is of terrible
slowness overtaking haste.

He topped the glass
wall that was not a wall but
a bubble of life,

a solitary enclave — and
the bubble burst.

He lies on the floor, overcome
by entropy out here, with his thoughts
of algae, fire, impossible

lungs. Horned snails
scale the glass behind him, their
skin translucent almost

as the glass or water, marking
a trail for whichever

might follow, escort
the newt to his death, at sea.

You take him in your hand, and
his body fits precisely
there among the lines. His

cleft tail flickers a final
time, like a scale of dead skin

in your palm. He feels
the warmth of your hand.

Your fingers burn
in the water but no breath
comes. You close

the tap. The silence then,
as though it had a right

to more. The silence — and
he dies in the warmth of your hand.

His mate lies still
and low now, alone among
the fronds. Motion, sound

are suspended inside the lines
of these glass slabs. The fish

will not approach her; they crowd
to one side of the pool; she will
not move from the veins of the leaf

that holds her
like a palm. She is hostile, she will
kill them. The turtles' blunt heads

butt the walls dumbly, again and yet
again, but even the water
draws back from her body.

This water no longer contains her.
Neither belongs. She is
free. She is waiting.

Time, silence, calm;
the architecture

of love. What to do
with the warm body in your hand.

For Blaise Cendrars

It is not so far. Three states, a hundred miles,
Two hours

Like changing cars in the middle of a trip:
Nothing more than that, nothing   .
More serious

Just to stand here
With a wife and a child of five years
Another woman in London (yes, Blaise,
We are very far from there; yes,
Jeanne, very far)
Whose belly would heave with my child
And one here whose
Won't, one with a still, flat belly

Falling away as I come into the street . . .

Young Negroes rustle cabs by the handle
For me
Follow one, running, down the block
Pull it down before me on the street
It exhudes a smell of urine or resignation

Again I am in the middle of a trip
Again I am changing cars

And here I am in my scattered bags
In a taxi
The words *Port* and *Authority* not wasted on me
Nor *Terminal*
Crouched in the antique doorway: yes, I know
On the sill
Like a moth, waiting

No, Chris, you won't be able to understand
Or even finally stand it
"Tell me, Jim —"
One cannot escape those implications

NATIONAL ACADEMY OF ARTISTS
IN WATERCOLOR
(above the aluminum front of a
travel agent in London)

That quiet, violent man knew it
He talked to a sleeping girl and told her
As I to an absent one now
Saying I was afraid, I couldn't
Go to the end
He was a bad poet returning to Paris
With fire and a little girl from Montmartre
He would like this city now
Where he wrote an Easter poem once
Nothing human was foreign to him
I've learned some stories, black as the paint
On the fire escape outside my window here

And they would appear in a book with his poems
I think we might have talked and got on
But I could pass him on the street
And never know, I would think: he belongs here

BEING DEMOLISHED
STARRING S&M DEMOLITION COMPANY
AN S&M PRODUCTION
GET YOUR FREE TICKETS INSIDE

The urge is to speak French, grope
For words in Spanish
This is the name for that
This is the way you ask for something
And I only understand part of it
Myself

I have established myself at the nearest bar
Order beer and leave large tips
Send flowers to the landlady
Uptown Negroes, queens, prostitutes
Around me on the street, walking home late

On the underground with Mike in his British accent
A young girl suffered seven years from a toy chair in
    her lung
In my furnished apartment I think of Thoreau
Or Tom last year in London
Learning to put their distress signals in code

I won't allow newspapers in the flat
I burned the last ones you brought
I wanted to tear them to shreds, open my window,
  I didn't

Afraid to go all the way
Like you, but for different reasons
And a bad poet too, *si mauvaise*
I think we could have talked and got along here
Sitting in the hips of these two cities
Two cowboys
Dan Yack and all the gold gone
All our money in the rum trade
Salvation between the legs of women

You wonder where your hand is
Little Jeanne asks, "Tell me, Blaise —"
We are both bad poets
We are both at the end, different ends
Or an edge
Nos dames naked and mad and upside-down in ruin
Renée asks, "Tell me —"
And we talk, together now

My fingers rise towards the sky
Inside Orion where it blazes and burns
They touch
Your own cold hand